TRANSFORMATIONAL
MINISTRY

TRANSFORMATIONAL MINISTRY

Church Leadership and the Way of the Cross

MICHAEL JINKINS

with a preface by Jeremy Begbie

SAINT ANDREW PRESS

For Robert M. Shelton

First published in 2002 by
SAINT ANDREW PRESS
121 George Street
Edinburgh EH2 4YN

Copyright © Michael Jinkins, 2002

ISBN 0 7152 0764 4

British Library Cataloguing in Publication Data
A catalogue record for this book is available from the British Library

Typeset in Times New Roman
Printed in Great Britain by Creative Print & Design, Wales

Contents

Contents

Preface

There are really only two kinds of books in my study: those I read once, and those to which I return repeatedly for wisdom and encouragement. Without a doubt, this book will belong to the second group.

Like Dr Jinkins, I have the privilege of teaching in a seminary. One of the commonest anxieties among students is the fear of losing their humanity. 'What about my hobbies and interests, my sense of humour and playfulness? What about the passions which have made me what I am? Am I going to be flattened into a "nice" person, easy-going but colourless and bland?' Michael Jinkins focuses our attention on the heart of the Christian faith: the astounding news of Jesus Christ is that God takes us on as we are so that we might become not less but *more* human, and that through us others may likewise discover their true human identity

And no-one needs to hear this more than a would-be minister. With acute clarity, Dr Jinkins exposes the shallowness of pragmatic, technique-centred concepts of ministry, where pastoring the people of God becomes little more than managing quick-fix schemes in the obsessive pursuit of relevance. This essentially dehumanises the pastor, turning him or her into a mechanical manager. It also dehumanises the congregation, who become little more than recipients of programmes. Without turning his back on the wealth of insight that the social and psychological sciences provide, Dr Jinkins sets ministry firmly within its proper theological environment – the spring of all fruitful ministry is sharing in the risen ministry of the crucified and risen Christ, in whose humanity our own is renewed. Very few books on ministry ever get around to saying this.

vii

Two other aspects of the book are especially unusual. First, you will find a remarkable range of sources here, including Barth, Calvin, Chrysostom, Gregory the Great, Herbert and Merton, not to mention a host of secular writers. Though firmly rooted in the Reformed tradition, Dr Jinkins rightly sees that a theology of ministry that cannot see beyond its familiar walls will be deeply impoverished. Second, though he only makes passing reference to this, Dr Jinkins has himself been a pastor and has known the struggles and exhilaration of this high calling from the inside. This is theology hammered out in the midst of blood-and-sweat experience.

This book is a jewel. You will return to it again and again for the joy of beholding the divine light refracted through it.

Dr Jeremy Begbie
Vice-Principal
Ridley Hall, Cambridge

Acknowledgements

This book would not have been possible without the cooperation, patience and insights of many people. The Master of Divinity students to whom I first delivered these lectures taught me far more than I taught them, and I can hear the voices of members of the churches I have served speaking on virtually every page. Anyone familiar with the thought of James B. Torrance, my teacher and mentor, will recognise his ideas throughout this book. I am also indebted to the thought of Murray Bowen, mediated through Edwin Friedman and Michael Kerr, and I hope that this brief book represents an original application of certain aspects of their work.

My colleagues at Austin Seminary have provided helpful reflections and critiques of this work as it has progressed, and have often sparked thoughts that were expanded in these pages. I am especially grateful to Stanley Hall, Scott Black Johnston and our friend and colleague the late Alan E. Lewis. Alan's belief that 'ministry is theology's polygraph' served as a guide and a goad in writing this book. I want to thank the Reverend Iain C. Barclay, an experienced minister, postgraduate researcher at the University of Aberdeen, and friend, who graciously worked through the manuscript and made numerous valuable editorial suggestions. I want to thank my secretary, Alison Riemersma, and research assistant, Carol Howard Merritt, for their assistance in preparing this book for press. I also want to thank my student assistants, Margaret Desmond and Patricia Felter, for proofreading the manuscript. As always, I am most grateful to Lesley Taylor and the team at Saint Andrew Press, both for the editorial vision and for the attention to detail which have become hallmarks of this press.

My thanks go, in particular, to Jeremy Begbie, Vice-Principal of Ridley Hall, Cambridge, for his preface to this book. Those who know Jeremy will share my enthusiasm for his theological reflections and his commitment to the ministry of teaching.

MICHAEL JINKINS
Austin Presbyterian Theological Seminary
Austin, Texas

Introduction

One of the faculty responsibilities I most enjoy is teaching senior divinity students a course entitled 'Entry into Ministry'. Taught, as it is, during the final term of the final year of academic work, just as students are preparing to leave the world of formal theological education to enter parish ministry, its discussions tend to be especially lively, fuelled by a combination of anxiety and zeal.

In a recent class discussion, a student mentioned a workshop she had attended in which an 'image consultant' spoke to the gathered ministers (or church professionals as they referred to themselves). The consultant pointed up the need for clergy to project a positive professional image. She told them that, because they are made in the image of God, they should buy only the best-quality clothes, jewellery and accessories, and should make every effort to look as chic and smart as possible. After the student related her (all-too-true) story, I paused for a very long time. I was frankly appalled and, momentarily, at a loss for words.

The students sat as the silence hung heavy around us. Finally, I said: 'I guess what I'm trying to picture in my mind is this: how should we look if we are supposed to reflect the image of the God who has revealed himself to us in the tormented shape of a Jewish man named Jesus, crucified on a city dump and discarded by the powers of his world?'

In the face of the daily trivialisation of virtually everything related to the Christian faith, this book seeks to address this and other questions related to the fundamental purpose of the Christian ministry. It seeks to put forward this thesis: *the purpose of our common ministry is the transformation of persons into the likeness of this Jesus Christ whom humanity crucified and God raised from the dead.* This book will focus primarily on the ministry of leadership engaged in by those who are ordained to pastoral ministry, though I hope it can also be of benefit to persons in other vocations.

We shall seek to understand what would be entailed in a pastoral ministry that reflects the character of the God who is revealed on the cross of Jesus Christ, asking:

- What does it mean to be a minister who does not hide from the painful actuality of the world, our own mixed motives, the vagaries of power and the conflicts of daily life?

- What would it require to be a minister aware of the profound complexity of human nature and human society, and (at the same time) to be a minister who is aware of the infinite complexity of the unconditional claim under which we have been laid by Jesus Christ?

- What are the barriers to a ministry that takes seriously the cross as the central transformative reality in human history?

My hope in writing this book is to open a larger conversation about vocational integrity in Christian ministry. My concern grows from a conviction that in the past half-century, while the influence of Christian ministry on the ways and means of the business and political world has diminished, the ways and means of the business and political world have made enormous inroads of influence into the ministry of the Church.

In the midst of ecclesiastical controversies over property claims, denominational structures, shrinking financial resources, human sexuality and a variety of more and less significant moral issues, mixed generously with bitter inter-tribal and regional rivalries, we have failed both to inspire and comfort, and to confront and challenge the world of persons around us. We have converted *stewardship* (the right use of all aspects of God's creation) into fund raising, *evangelism* (the joyful announcement of God's grace) into recruitment, and *justice* (the distribution among all persons of God's love) into a political end in itself.

We ask, 'Why do so few people want to join with us in the Church?'

The real question is: 'Why indeed should they?!'

Our essential mission, as George MacLeod told us forty years ago, is 'to be to others what Christ has become for us'. '*And what,*' we may ask, 'has Christ – this man acquainted with sorrow in whose stripes we are healed – *become for us?*'

He has become death for us. He has taken into himself the tormented shape of our sin, our in-dependence, our dis-ease and dis-grace, and, as St Paul tells us, he has left all this inhumanity nailed to the cross. This is *the death of death in the death of Christ,* of which the Puritan preacher John Owen spoke. It constitutes the most profound and the most neglected message at the heart of the good news of Jesus Christ, a message that our fearful and grieving, yet death-denying, culture needs to hear.

Jesus Christ has also become life for us, creative life, risen life, brilliant, shining, unending life, 'full of grace and truth'. Christ, dead and discarded by the world, has been raised by God to the position of honour and power above every earthly power. In so doing, God places his seal of approval upon the whole life of Jesus, as if to say, *This crucified life is the life for which humanity was designed. Go and do likewise.* The death we fear so desperately that we become unable to live does not have the last word. The last word is God's Word, God's creative Word, which has the power to bring creation out of nothing, the power to raise every death to new life.

This is what *we say* we believe. And so we do.

The question we ask in these pages is: 'How, on the basis of this belief, can we also say that Christ provides our model for ministry, ministry in the way of the cross, not a ministry merely of vested interest and jealous professionalism, but ministry that is poured out without reservation in the hope that God will provide what is needed, in the incredible hope that we can be partners with God in God's miraculous work of transforming persons!'

St Paul articulates a model for ministry that takes these questions seriously, when he writes:

> I urge you therefore, brothers and sisters, by the mercies of God, to offer your lives as a living and holy sacrifice, acceptable to God. This is your spiritual service of worship. And do not allow yourself to be conformed to this world, but be transformed by the renewing of your mind, that you may demonstrate what God's will is, that which is good and acceptable and whole. (Romans 12:1–2)

Our challenge, of course, is to minister as though we believed that this is not only true, *but also real.*

O Lord Jesus Christ, give us thy blessing in our preparation for the work for the ministry in thy holy church. Remove far from us the spirit of worldliness and give us grace, that we may continually grow in that holiness of life which is required of those who bear the vessels of the Lord. Give us that wisdom which comes from above, and that gentleness which becomes the gospel of peace. Make us diligent in the study of thy Word, and teach us by thy Spirit so that we may be enabled to teach others . . . , doing all things unto thy glory, who with the Father and the Holy Ghost are one God, world without end. Amen.

John Wright (altered)

1

Character

has Priority over Technique

Therefore,
since we have been justified through faith,
we have peace with God
through Jesus Christ,
through whom we have gained access by faith
into this grace in which we now stand.
And we rejoice in the hope of the glory of
God.
Not only so, but we also rejoice in our
sufferings,
because we know that suffering produces
perseverance;
perseverance, character;
and character, hope.
And hope does not disappoint us, because
God has poured out his love into our hearts
by the Holy Spirit, whom he has given us.

Romans 5:1–5 (New International Version)

If we were to walk into any bookshop that caters for the needs of Christian clergy and congregations and were to go to the section of resources that focuses on ministry and the life of the congregation, we would find a large proportion of books dedicated to developing better 'techniques' or 'methods' in various areas of concern such as preaching, counselling and administration. Typically, these resources provide what we might call

'Pastoral DIY', and, like the 'Do it yourself' books we find on gardening and woodworking, they would be full of step-by-step procedures and lists of suggestions, helpful hints and sometimes advice worth taking. The problem with these resources is simply this: *unless* the minister is already grounded in that which is essential to pastoral ministry, *all the good advice in the world won't matter*; it won't help; it won't contribute to the long-term health of either the minister or the Church.

'And what is it that is essential to pastoral ministry?' Simply this: coming to terms with who we are as persons and ministers, which includes the following: (1) *our pastoral identity*, our understanding of what it means to be a particular kind of leader (a leader who leads as Minister of Word and Sacrament) among the people of God; (2) *our sense of personal authenticity*, of character and humility, integrity and strength, which undergirds and fills with moral significance our leadership in the congregation; and (3) *a genuine spirituality* (to use the word most often used these days) *or piety* (to use the word favoured in our own Reformed tradition), which is the gift of God through Christ by the power of the Holy Spirit, a piety grounded in the life, worship and devotion of the community under the guidance of the Word of God. Whereas some personal technologians, following in the tradition of Simon Magus (see Acts, chapter 8), may give us the impression that professionalism and vocational competency are based on the successful exercise of various methods of Church management or techniques in Church growth (as though we were saying that our ability to exercise professional skills defines our ministry and justifies our being pastors), *the tradition in which we stand says that our profession is given to us by the God who calls us*.

This is at the heart of what we mean by vocation, from the Latin *vocatio*, to call. In fact, the only thing that sustains our call is the creative breath of God on which that call is carried from the Word of God through the Body of Christ to our listening ears. This call finds resonance in us because the God who formed us out of nothing, the God who has reformed us in a community of persons, informs us now that our identity corresponds to God's purpose for us. We were created for *this* design, or even *this*. What is 'fitting' for us is so because we were cut out by God for it. God's calling of us, so to speak, tells us who we are.

We are *who we are* by the grace of God. And, because we understand who we are in relation to this God, we live the way we do, and act the way we do, we have certain gifts and interests, and we practise ministry the way we do, *instead of some other way*. Various professional techniques may be helpful to the minister who must strive for competence and excellence, but no technique in the world can substitute for the identity provided by God's call and the character which is instilled by God's spirit as we yield to God's leadership over our lives.

As ministers we are tested as metal in a fire. And as the integrity of metal is tried under stress, flaws in our character will become apparent in the stress of pastoral leadership. We pray not for techniques that will tide us over or help us to hide our weaknesses. Rather, we pray for forgiveness when we fail, grace that will uphold us and the power of God to shape in us the character of God revealed in Christ.

In other words, we believe that character has priority over techniques. This essential issue of pastoral ministry relates to other fundamental convictions running through all of human life:

> *Philosophically*, we affirm that ontology (being) is prior to economy (doing).
> *Grammatically*, we say that the indicative gives rise to the imperative.
> *Biblically* and *theologically*, we confess that grace gives us the Law (Torah).

Thus Calvin prays:

> Enlighten us, O God, by your Spirit, in the understanding of your Word, and grant us the grace to receive it in wonder and humility, that we may learn to put our trust in you, to reverence and honour you, by glorifying your Holy Name in all our life, and to yield you our love and obedience. Amen.
>
> John Calvin

2

Our Model for Ministry

The High Priesthood of Christ

Every high priest is selected from among
men and is appointed
to represent them in matters related to God
to offer gifts and sacrifices for sins.
He is able to deal gently with those who are
ignorant and going astray, since he himself
is subject to weakness. This is why he has to
offer sacrifices for his own sins, as well as for
the sins of the people.
No-one takes this honor upon himself; he
must be called by God, just as Aaron was.

Hebrews 5:1–5 (New International Version)

In order to get at the heart of Christian ministry, we shall begin with John Calvin's discussion of the High Priesthood of Jesus Christ. There is much to learn from the Reformer about what it means to share in God's ministry of transformation. In the light of what we will find in Calvin, we will then be able to understand the theological significance of the minister's work (in ministry, worship and preaching) as placing ourselves at God's disposal as God seeks to transform persons through the renewing of their minds into the likeness of Jesus Christ.

John Calvin had the most remarkable habit of speaking of human ministry always in the light of the ministry of Jesus Christ. He highlights the fact that we do not perform our ministry in isolation as though it is something we produce, something we can be proud of, something that depends on *our* strength and intelligence and skills. There is a restful quality to Calvin's discussions of our ministry, a restful, trustful quality grounded in the awareness that our ministry is given to us by God; and that which God gives, God empowers.

The success of our ministry does not depend on us. Our ministry and, indeed, our entire lives are in God's hands, as though we are tools in the hands of a skilled carpenter. And, while we are responsible to be good tools, the work is not accomplished because of our sharpness. God accomplishes God's ministry with even the dullest of tools.

The key to understanding Calvin's restfulness and trustfulness, his lack of anxiety, lies in his view of Christ as our heavenly high priest, as we see in his commentary of the Epistle to the Hebrews. Hebrews reads:

> Since, then, we have a great high priest who has passed through the heavens, Jesus, the Son of God, let us hold fast to our confession. For we do not have a high priest who is unable to sympathise with our weaknesses, but we have one who in every respect has been tested as we are, yet without sin. Let us therefore approach the throne of grace with boldness, so that we may receive mercy and find grace to help in time of need. (4:14–16, New Revised Standard Version)

Calvin discusses this passage in one of the finest commentaries to emerge from the Protestant Reformation. He writes:

> The apostle [intended] . . . only to teach us that since Christ holds out His hand to us we have no need to look for a mediator far off: that there is no reason for us to fear the majesty of Christ, since He is our Brother; and that we must not be afraid that He is unaware of our ills and not touched by any feeling of humanity to bring us help, since He has taken our infirmities on Himself so as to be better able to help us.[1]

We are to approach the throne of grace, Calvin continues, 'with boldness', because the throne of God is not marked by a naked majesty which overpowers us, but is adorned with a new name, that of grace . . . The sum of all this is that we may safely call on God, since we know that He is propitious to us. This happens because of the mercy of Christ, as is stated in Ephesians 3:12, because when Christ accepts us into His faith and discipleship, He covers with His goodness the majesty of God which could otherwise be fearful, so that nothing appears except grace and fatherly goodwill.[2]

According to Calvin, *Jesus Christ's high priestly ministry has two complementary aspects, both of which have fundamental implications for pastoral ministry.* First, *Christ presents us, in his own person, to God the Father.* In the person of Christ, we are brought (even now!) into the very presence of God. As Jeremy Begbie has said, calling to remembrance the figure of the High Priest in ancient Judaism, Christ comes into the presence of God the Father *with our names carved upon his heart.*

Our needs, our pain, all that we hope *and* fear, our most exquisite joys and longings, our alienation, and ultimately even our death, are brought into God's presence through the intercession of Christ, who, Calvin says, 'has taken our infirmities on Himself so as to be able to help us'.

As our needs and sufferings, hopes and fears are brought to God through Christ, even so they are transformed in Christ; as we pray *through Christ* we find ourselves changed. Some things we feared, as we commit them to God, lose their terror. Some things we had hoped, as we bring them under the scrutiny of God's hope in Christ, may be found to be unworthy of 'hope', and so we exchange our shabby hope for God's own.

'There is a communion with God', wrote George MacDonald, 'that asks for nothing, yet asks for everything . . . He [*sic*] who seeks the Father more than anything He can give, is likely to have what he asks, for he is not likely to ask amiss.' This is in part what it means to pray 'in the name of Jesus Christ', to allow Christ to transform our prayers to correspond to God's will for us. Thus to pray without ceasing means to live, in Christ, as one who is being transformed.

The second aspect of Christ's high priestly ministry is *his sharing of God's ministry with us by the power of the Spirit*. Even as Christ presents us to God in himself, so also Christ shares with us the Spirit who gives us the power to repent, to turn towards God so that we can reflect on our own faces the radiance of God's glory. We come actually to participate in the ministry of Christ, to share, by the Spirit of Christ, *his love* which casts out fear and *his trust* which casts out anxiety, *his allegiance* to the kingly rule of God in all of life and *his courage* to follow at all costs. *Christ shares with us who he is.*

Calvin, in his *Institutes*, says that, while we 'are defiled in ourselves, yet are [we] priests in him'. In Christ, we 'offer ourselves and our all to God, and freely enter the heavenly sanctuary that the sacrifices of prayer and praise that we bring may be acceptable and sweet-smelling before God'. 'This', Calvin says, 'is the meaning of Christ's statement: "For their sake I sanctify myself" [John 17:19]. For we, imbued with his holiness in so far as he has consecrated us to the Father with himself, although we would otherwise be loathsome to him, please him as pure and clean – and even as holy.'[3]

Jesus Christ takes into himself our dis-ease and dis-grace and gives us, in return, his restful trust in God. 'Now we see how Christ is the most perfect image of God', Calvin says; 'if we are conformed to it, we are so restored that with true piety, righteousness, purity and intelligence we bear God's image.' And this image which we bear is the likeness of Jesus Christ whose entire life was offered without reservation to God, with complete confidence in God. 'What was primary in the renewing of God's image,' he says, 'also held the highest place in the creation itself. To the same pertains what [St Paul] teaches elsewhere, that "we . . . with unveiled face beholding the glory of Christ are being transformed into his very image" [2 Corinthians 3:18].'[4]

Ministry that is cognisant of the continuing priestly work of Christ can share, by the power of the Holy Spirit, in God's transformative power, the power to be present, to stand by, to wait and trust in God beyond the contingencies of this life. We are aware that our deepest needs and the needs of those we serve are brought into the presence of God by one who can be trusted to do for us 'better things than we can desire or pray for'.[5]

Calvin's comments on the Epistle to the Hebrews lead us to St Paul's Epistle to the Ephesians and, consequently, to Calvin's commentary on Ephesians. The section of Ephesians, to which Calvin refers, reads as follows:

> Of this gospel I have become a servant according to the gift of God's grace, that was given me by the working of his power. Although I am the very least of all the saints, this grace was given to me to bring to the Gentiles the news of the boundless riches of Christ, and to make everyone see what is the plan of the mystery hidden for ages in God who created all things; so that through the church the wisdom of God in its rich variety might now he made known to the rulers and authorities in the heavenly places. This was in accordance with the eternal purpose that he has carried out in Christ Jesus our Lord, in whom we have access to God in boldness and confidence through faith in him. I pray therefore that you may not lose heart over my sufferings for you; they are your glory.
>
> For this reason I bow my knees before the Father, from whom every family in heaven and on earth takes its name. I pray that, according to the riches of his glory, he may grant that you may be strengthened in your inner being with power through his Spirit, and that Christ may dwell in your hearts through faith, as you are being rooted and grounded in love. I pray that you may have the power to comprehend with all the saints, what is the breadth and length and height and depth, and to know the love of Christ that surpasses knowledge, so that you may be filled with all the fullness of God.
>
> Now to him who by the power at work within us is able to accomplish abundantly far more than all we can ask or imagine, to him be glory in the church and in Christ Jesus to all generations, forever and ever. Amen. (Ephesians 3:7–20, NRSV)

Calvin comments on this passage:

> Those who separate faith from confidence are like men [*sic*] trying to take heat or light from the sun. I acknowledge, indeed, that, in proportion to the measure of faith, confidence is small in some and greater in others; but faith will never be found without these effects or fruits. A trembling, hesitating, doubting conscience will always be a sure proof of unbelief; but a firm, steady conscience, victorious against the gates of hell, will be the sure proof of faith. To trust in Christ as Mediator, and to rest with assurance in God's fatherly love, to dare boldly to promise ourselves eternal life, and not to tremble at death or hell, this is, as they say, a holy presumption . . .[6]
>
> Now you see why he [St Paul] had earlier mentioned his chains. It was to prevent them [the Ephesians] from being discouraged when they heard of his persecution. O heroic heart, which drew from prison and death itself, comfort for those who were not in danger! He remembers his *tribulations* for the Ephesians, because they brought edification for all the godly. How powerfully is the faith of the people confirmed, when a pastor does not hesitate to seal his doctrine by the surrender of his life! And accordingly he adds, *which is your glory*. His preaching was so lustred, that all the churches among whom he had taught had good reason to glory that their faith was ratified by the best of all pledges.[7]

Commenting on the following section of this passage, Calvin counters the view of some opponents who, in Calvin's opinion, focused so much on their own activity, on the things they claimed to produce and made to happen, that they were unable to hear the message that *God alone produces in us all things that are pleasing to God.*

Calvin makes clear that every true teaching and every faithful act of ministry is produced in us by the Holy Spirit. He writes: 'Therefore the Lord alone acts upon us in such a way that He acts by His own instruments. It is therefore the duty of pastors diligently to teach, of people earnestly to attend to teaching, and of both, to flee to the Lord lest they weary themselves in unprofitable exertions.'[8]

In his comments on St Paul's beautiful doxology, Calvin draws together his fullest thought on the Christian life:

> Paul . . . does not wish the saints to be strengthened so that they may excel and flourish in the world, but that, with respect to the Kingdom of God, their souls may be strong with the power of God . . . For since the Father placed in Christ the fullness of all gifts, so he who has Christ dwelling in him can want nothing. They are mistaken who hope the Spirit can be obtained apart from obtaining Christ; and they are equally foolish and absurd who dream that Christ can be received without the Spirit. Both must be believed. We are partakers of the Holy Spirit to the extent that we share in Christ; for the Spirit will be found nowhere but in Christ, on whom He is said to have rested for that purpose. Nor can Christ be separated from the Spirit; for then He would be, so to say, dead, and empty of His power. Paul well defines those who are endowed with the spiritual power of God as those in Whom Christ dwells. Also, he points out that part which is the true seat of Christ, our hearts, to show that it is not enough for Him to be on our tongues or flutter in our brains.

The substance of our faith, our personal trust, in Christ 'is that Christ is not to be viewed from afar by faith, but to be received by the embrace of our minds, so that He may dwell in us, and so it is that we are filled with the Spirit of God'.[9]

In a passage characteristically Calvinist, though the authorship is in doubt, the end, or goal, of Christian ministry is seen as a kind of channel through which God, 'the founder of all felicity', flows to all humanity, communicating 'Christ to us who are disunited by sin and hence ruined, that we may from him enjoy eternal life, that . . . all heavenly treasures be so applied to us that they be no less ours than Christ's himself'.[10]

I want us to direct our attention to a few of Calvin's most trenchant observations in these passages, listening especially to what Calvin teaches us about Christian ministry as participation in God's transformation of persons.

First, in order to understand who we are, Calvin tells us, we must direct our attention away from ourselves to Jesus Christ. Focusing on ourselves, we do not see our true humanity. But, by the power of the Holy Spirit, through faith, we glimpse in Jesus Christ who we are, the true humanity for which God created us. Under the Spirit's tutelage, we hear and learn from the Word of God our rightful, proper name, the name by which God knows and calls us, *the name given us in Jesus Christ.* Being named by God after Christ, and united to Christ by God's grace, we are given a new humanity that has been beyond our experience, scarcely imaginable to us 'who are disunited by sin and hence ruined'.[11] And yet we recognise that the humanity of Jesus Christ is so truly our humanity that we know ourselves as ourselves in him only when we hear this name uttered by the Word and given to us by the Spirit.

The humanity of Jesus Christ constitutes a life lived in utter dependence upon God the Father, a life of simple trust in God, a life that derives its power, its strength, its comfort, its security, from God alone. This life is none other than the life Jesus lived in the power of the Spirit and which the Spirit shares with us now. Paradoxically, then, we do not know ourselves by fixing our vision on ourselves, on our behaviour, or feelings, or attitudes. We find ourselves, our identity, the meaning of our humanity and, in fact, the meaning of our ministry by looking (through the power of the Spirit) to Jesus Christ, 'the mirror of our sanctification'. We know who we are by virtue of our union with Christ.

Second, even as the meaning of our ministry derives from Christ, so also the shape and effectiveness of our ministry is given to us by Christ through God's Spirit. Our ministry is not something we define and accomplish and then present to God as *our* achievement.

Again, the source of ministry lies in our spiritual union with Christ, by which we share in his ministry through the Spirit. Jesus Christ is the heavenly high priest, the true pastor, the curate of all souls, the true

Minister of Word and Sacrament, the leader of our worship and the constant mediator who intercedes for us in the presence of God the Father.

Our ministry participates, by the power of God's Spirit, in the ministry of Christ, because we have been united with Christ, 'not', Calvin says, 'in an imaginary way, but most powerfully and truly, so that we become flesh of his flesh and bone of his bone'.[12]

Third, we come to an understanding of grace, peace and comfort, we come to understand what we value and love and hope, through tribulations and trials, as God shares with us God's own strength to endure through God's Spirit. The resilience and persistence necessary for Christian ministry, the personal confidence in God that dispels anxiety and makes it possible for us to live among those we serve, while not becoming merely a transmitter for their anxiety, are given to us as we pass through the fire of conflict and difficulties relying on God for God's strength.

By the *'vivifying flesh' of Jesus Christ*, Calvin says, *God 'transfuses eternal life into us'*. Distress is not an end in itself because, united with Christ, we are united in his suffering, a suffering that has its goal and finds its ultimate meaning in the gracious heart of God.[13]

'Hence,' writes Calvin, 'also in harsh and difficult conditions, regarded as adverse and evil, a great comfort comes to us: we share Christ's sufferings in order that as he has passed from a labyrinth of all evils into heavenly glory, we may in like manner be led through various tribulations to the same glory.' We endure because we are expectant – *not optimistic*, as though circumstances might simply get better on their own – *but hopeful*, trusting the future, our future, to God. The God-given endurance which is perhaps the most important element in our pastoral leadership is shown to us in Christ, whose whole life, as Calvin said, 'was nothing but a sort of perpetual cross'.[14] Our endurance of the cross in all of life is the sermon that underlies every sermon we hope to preach. We shall examine this more closely in the following sections.

Finally, we rest in God's power (the particular kind of power God demonstrates on the cross by which God announces his judgement on what we commonly call power). We are not anxious about what may or may not happen. *We* are unafraid in the face of difficulties and distress, and we are able to hear criticism, because we already know ourselves to be frail and fallible, in need of grace and forgiveness. We rest in the hands of God as we seek to build up and bring health to God's people. This is the first thing we must learn if our ministry is to share the way of the cross.

Notes

1. John Calvin, *The Epistle of St. Paul the Apostle to the Hebrews and the First and Second Epistles of St. Peter*, trans. William B. Johnston, *Calvin's Commentaries*, ed. David W. Torrance and Thomas F. Torrance (Grand Rapids: Eerdmans, 1963), XII.55.
2. Ibid., XII.56–7.
3. John Calvin, *Institutes of the Christian Religion*, ed. John T. McNeill, trans. Ford Lewis Battles (Philadelphia: Westminster Press, 1960).
4. Ibid., I.xv.4.
5. *Book of Common Prayer*, According to the Use of the Protestant Episcopal Church in the United States of America (New York: Church Pension Fund, 1945), 597.
6. John Calvin, *The Epistles of Paul the Apostle to the Galatians, Ephesians, Philippians and Colossians*, trans. T. H. L. Parker, *Calvin's Commentaries*, ed. David W. Torrance and Thomas F. Torrance (Grand Rapids: Eerdmans, 1965), XI.164.
7. Ibid., XI.165.
8. Ibid., XI.165–6.
9. Ibid., XI.169–70.
10. Calvin, *Theological Treatises*, ed. J. K. S. Reid (Philadelphia: Westminster Press, 1954), 171.
11. Ibid., 171.
12. Ibid., 171–2.
13. Ibid., 171.
14. Calvin, *Institutes*, III.viii.1.

Grant me, I beseech thee, O merciful God, ardently to desire, prudently to study, rightly to understand, and perfectly to fulfil that which is pleasing to thee, to the praise and glory of thy name. Amen.

Thomas Aquinas

3

On a Mission from God

Clarity of Purpose

In *The Blues Brothers*, a comedy film of some years ago, Jake and Elwood, two blues musicians, went in search of their old band members so they could put on a charity concert to save the parochial school they attended as young juvenile delinquents. While they were visiting a Black congregation on the south side of Chicago, they experienced a very funny epiphany that confirmed to them the divine origin of their mission. From that moment on, as they went from door to door tracking down their former band members, they told people: 'We're on a mission from God.'

I wish we all possessed such clarity of purpose. Clarity of purpose is essential for a minister. You may remember Ross Perot, the Texan billionaire Presidential candidate, whose running mate in the 1992 vice-presidential debates began his prepared statement with the words: 'Who am I? Why am I here?' These are the questions each of us must answer in order to be faithful ministers. *Who am I? Why am I here?*

The first concerns that face us are not concerns over professional methods and techniques (important as these are), but personal character and vocational identity. We need to reflect on the fundamental questions of character and identity:

- In light of who God has revealed Godself to be in Christ, *what does it mean to be created in the image of God*?

- In light of the true humanity revealed in Jesus Christ, *what does it mean to be human*?

15

- In light of the ministry of Jesus Christ, what does it mean to be called by Christ to serve as his minister?

These are the issues, as Dietrich Bonhoeffer has said, which are central to Christian theology *and* human existence. As the editor of Bonhoeffer's lectures on Christology writes,

> Bonhoeffer is not prepared to find a category for Christ. His questions are not, 'How is it possible for Christ to be both man and God?' His question about Christ is never 'How?' but always 'Who?' . . . Every avenue of his thinking leads him to confront Christ and ask, 'Who art thou, Lord?' or to be confronted by Christ and hear his question, 'Who do you say that I am?'[1]

To be ministers, it is essential that we face the question of being. Otherwise, we are swept along by the current of largely irrelevant questions and the vacuous answers that ultimately lead to exhaustion and meaninglessness. We are surrounded by instances of the vanity that empties ministry of its vitality and force. We commonly call this vanity by the popular name 'burnout'; but the name fails to convey the profound spiritual crisis experienced by those who find themselves unable to continue in ministry because their resources are spent, or by those who continue to occupy the office long after the passion for ministry has evaporated.

The neo-Pelagianism that sees ministry as our product, to which we alluded in our reflections on the High Priesthood of Christ, has this end, to lead ministers into the vanity (a term which includes both *emptiness* and *arrogance*) of thinking of themselves as the producers of ministry on whose shoulders rest ministry's success and effectiveness.[2] The alternative, as we have already made clear, is to actively rest in God's power – not in our own – through the power of the Spirit, to make and to do that which is pleasing to God because it is God's own making and doing. What the term 'burnout' cannot convey sufficiently is the vain emptiness of an entire culture that is directed towards self-aggrandisement, self-congratulation and the arrogance of believing that we have the resources to fulfil the needs of others.

This leads us to a question of extraordinary significance:

Who or what determines the scope and content of our ministry?
A job description?
The latest management theory?
The vote of the congregation or the governing body of the church?
Or is there something deeper going on?

Vanity feeds on popular acclaim. But it feeds in the way a black hole feeds, drawing in energy, consuming all that comes within its gravitational pull. What happens when the popular acclaim turns from thunderous applause to deafening silence? Is there a deeper source for vocational mission?

There is.

We need the clarity to be able to say (and to mean): 'I'm on a mission from God.' God is the source and Godself the defining criteria for this mission. And what is the nature of this mission? St Paul says the mission is the building-up (edification) of the body of Christ. This is the power which defies vanity and gives new fire to those who are 'burned out'.

In the Epistle to the Romans, St Paul describes what this building-up looks like:

> I appeal to you therefore, brothers and sisters, by the mercies of God to present your bodies as a living sacrifice, holy and acceptable to God, which is your spiritual worship. Do not be conformed to this world, but be transformed by the renewing of your minds, so that you may discern what is the will of God – what is good and acceptable and perfect. (12:1–2, NRSV)

As ministers, we are letting go of ourselves, placing ourselves at God's disposal, as God seeks to transform persons through the renewing of their minds into the likeness of Christ. We are submitting ourselves to God's transforming power, asking God, by the power of God's Spirit, under the tutelage of Christ, to renew our own minds into the likeness of Christ. We who hope to share in Christ's ministry of transformation, to offer ourselves to be transformed by Christ.

Thus we are sent out into the life of the Church in the world to follow Christ and to lead others into the fellowship of Christ. Our first priority isn't simply to make meetings run well, to organise exciting programmes and lead stimulating worship; our first order of business is not to master a variety of techniques and methods to these tasks; our goal isn't to keep ourselves fired up or rested up to prevent professional burnout. Rather, our first priority is to be present in the life of the Church and to lead in and through the life of the Church in such a way that every human endeavour may be understood as an occasion for God to work towards God's goal of transforming people through the renewing of their minds into the likeness of Christ. The services, activities, the meetings and programmes are never ends in themselves but are merely occasions for the transformation of persons, and this transformation is by God's own ministry in which we participate by God's Spirit.

St Paul, in Romans 12:3, lays down the fundamentals of Christian leadership. Notice where he starts: 'by the grace given to me I say to everyone among you not to think more highly of yourselves than you ought to think'. Our trust in God makes it possible for us to avoid taking ourselves too seriously, to help each of us to remember that *I am not the whole Body of Christ and the Kingdom of God does not depend on my efforts.* G. K. Chesterton once remarked that the reason angels can fly is because they take themselves so lightly.[3] God wants to achieve God's purposes in the world by empowering each member of the Body of Christ. This requires that we trust God a lot more than we trust ourselves. To put it another way, we'll never really get off the ground as long as we think it depends on us.

Not long ago, I had the opportunity to study with Edwin Friedman, the author of the well-known study of congregational life in churches and synagogues, *Generation to Generation*.[4] One thing he emphasised more than any other was that the most important characteristics of the congregational leader are a *non-anxious presence and clarity of purpose*. When we reflect on St Paul's understanding of Christian ministry, we see precisely this.

Do we hear the restfulness coming through St Paul's teachings? There's not a trace of anxiety here.

Do we hear the clarity of purpose, the clear articulation of vision? He is on a mission from God. He is at God's disposal to assist in any way he can in the building-up of the people of God.

Have we noticed how little St Paul dwells on what is wrong or frightening? He attacks failure sharply, clearly and unambiguously. But he doesn't dwell there.

In his letter to the Galatians, he says that we are called to freedom; but freedom doesn't lead to self-indulgence. Instead of biting and devouring one another, St Paul says, we are to 'live by the Spirit' and receive from God the fruit of God's Spirit, 'love, joy, peace, kindness, generosity, faithfulness, gentleness, and self-control. There is no law against such things.' Those who belong to Christ Jesus, St Paul says, 'have crucified the flesh [Paul's term for the unhumanity which runs counter to the Spirit] with its passions and desires'. That which is contrary to God and contrary to life has no real power; it is dead (Galatians 5:13ff. and 22ff.).

- Ministers who lead well (if we are to take Paul at his word) do not work out of their own anxiety, but out of their trust in God; they don't feed the frenzied anxiety of society (even when the frenzy of anxiety infects their congregation), but *speak calmly and clearly the Word of grace and peace*. They can only do this, they can only retain their sanity and balance and peace, *because they have entrusted their own lives, the lives of those they love, and the lives of their enemies, to the God who desires better things than we can desire.*

• Ministers who lead well also know that *conflict is not an evil to be avoided at all cost but is a gift from God which helps us clarify our own trust in God and which can contribute to the development of personal resources of resilience, strength and persistence.*

Thomas à Kempis (1380–1471) understood this. In what remains one of the most important classics of pastoral formation, his *Imitation of Christ*, he writes:

> *It is good for us to encounter troubles and adversities from time to time*, for trouble often compels a man [*sic*] to search his own heart. It reminds him that he is an exile here, and that he can put his trust in nothing in this world. *It is good, too, that we sometimes suffer opposition*, and that men think ill of us, even when we do and mean well. Such things are an aid to humility, and preserve us from pride and vainglory. For we more readily turn to God as our inward witness, when men despise us and think no good of us. *A man should therefore place such complete trust in God that he has no need of comfort from men.*[5]

And, again, he says: 'My will is that you do not try to find a place free from temptations and troubles. Rather, seek a peace that endures even when you are beset by various temptations and tried by much adversity.'[6]

Notes

1. Dietrich Bonhoeffer, *Christ the Center*, ed. John Bowden, 'Editorial Introduction' (New York: Harper & Row, 1960), 17.
2. The converse of this misconception of ministry is that it tends to see members of the congregation as consumers, a dehumanising of persons into mere passive receptors of ministerial programmes and activities.

3. G. K. Chesterton, *Orthodoxy* (London: The Bodley Head, 1908), 221.
4. Edwin H. Friedman, *Generation to Generation* (New York/London: Guildford Press, 1985). Also of value is *Friedman's Fables* (New York/London: Guildford Press, 1990). Also of interest in this context is Michael E. Kerr, 'Chronic Anxiety and Defining the Self', *The Atlantic* (September 1988), 35–58.
5. Thomas à Kempis, *The Imitation of Christ*, trans. with introduction by Leo Sherley-Price (London: Penguin, 1952), I.12.
6. Ibid., III.12.

4

Conflict

and the Ministry of Hope

Thou alone art the End of all good things,
the fullness of life,
the depth of wisdom;
and the greatest comfort of Thy servants is to
trust in Thee above all else.

Thomas à Kempis

Human life is essentially conflictual. From birth until death, we are shaped by the conflicts we face and by the way we face them. As Christians, far from escaping conflict, we are compelled to come to terms with it, not least because we believe that God has truly and fully revealed Godself in the tormented shape of the crucified Christ. Conflict is not only woven into the fabric of our existence, it is also essential to our calling as followers of Jesus.

The author of the Epistle of James tells us that we should 'consider it all joy' whenever we encounter various trials, knowing that the testing of our faith produces endurance. And if we persist in enduring, finally, we shall become complete, whole and perfect, all we are meant to be (James 1:2–4). These are statements of faith which enshrine a belief most of us find singularly unattractive, that conflict is essential to the development of Christian character. But if it is true, then we must – if we are to be true to our calling – learn *to minister through conflict*.

What I intend to suggest by this phrase, *to minister through conflict*, is something qualitatively different from what is conventionally called 'conflict resolution' or 'conflict management'. And the difference lies in a theological issue of the greatest significance, the Christian doctrine of hope.

The Church, St Paul says, is 'the Body of Christ', of which Christ himself is 'the Head'. Those who are members of the Church are so by virtue of the fact that they are 'called out' by the Word of God to live consciously and joyfully under the reign of God in the world. The Church is not the voluntary society of like-minded individuals which John Locke envisaged. It is, by very definition, a pluralistic 'Body', which is what it is because God has chosen to make it so. By virtue of the Church's identity and its vocation, it participates in what Jürgen Moltmann describes as a kind of 'messianic mediation' between the 'Kingdom of God' (God's unambiguous reign) and 'history' (the ambiguous realm of human endeavour). 'The Church is Christian', Moltmann has said, 'when, and to the extent in which, its mediations take their bearings from the history of Jesus and his mission.'[1] *If our ministry is to be Christian, then, we must have a particular relationship to conflict, a relationship defined by the life of this Jesus who was crucified and raised from the dead.*

As followers of Christ, we recognise that conflict is potentially redemptive and transformative. Thus, our perspective on conflict is not merely past-oriented, an attempt to return to a previous equilibrium, as implied in the term 'conflict resolution'. We are aware that much of that which is redemptive and transformative to persons could be lost to them if they returned to 'the way things were before this happened'. Whatever 'this' was, it has happened, and it is now a fact that is part of our history and which can enrich our experience. Any attempt to go behind it, to some pre-conflictual life, is an attempt to remove ourselves from history as a living force and to place ourselves in a *pseudo*-history that is static and, we suppose, safe (though even this safety is an illusion). 'Conflict resolution', in the way we are using the phrase, speaks to the human impulse to return to a garden of innocence. But, as we are all too aware, the way back to such a garden is blocked by a God who loves us enough to station in our path angels with flaming swords who will prevent our return.

A second approach to dealing with conflict, and one which also attracts us, is the present-oriented 'conflict management', which attempts to maintain a present comfort level or status quo. *Control is the key to this approach*: control over discomfort and disorientation, control of disagreement, control of dis-ease (which is not the same thing as health). The unstated assumption is that we have already attained to *all we are ever going to be*. We have already arrived. So, the ultimate goal of the Christian community is to preserve us where we are and to shelter us from threats of change. Any deviation from the present norms signals the disintegration of community. Thus conflicts are 'managed'. Damage is controlled, or, at least, the *appearance* of damage is *apparently* controlled. But appearances are deceiving.

Both of these approaches to conflict are based on the rather pessimistic assessment which surveys human experience and says that we are never likely to get any better than we now are, and could get a lot worse. The alternative to these approaches to conflict is no more optimistic. It recognises fully the dangers inherent in conflict, but it is hopeful (not optimistic) in that it is open-ended towards the living presence and promise of God. It anticipates God's redemptive work among us, which is, as Moltmann says, 'a fragment of the coming whole'. We refer to this alternative as 'ministry through conflict', a quality of ministry grounded in hope, ever watchful for what God is doing among us and through us.

Karl Barth, in a brief exposition of 1 John 3:2, describes this hope. He comments on the passage: 'Beloved, now we are children of God, and it has not appeared as yet what we shall be. We know that, when He appears, we shall be like Him, because we shall see Him just as He is. And every one who has this hope fixed on Him purifies himself, just as He is pure.' As we look around us in the church, at the conflicts that embroil us, we may well ask: 'What is the point?' Perhaps God is working among us, but our possibilities are veiled; we may look for God's transformative

workmanship in the faces of those who press against us, though we cannot
see clearly; it is as though we are looking 'through a mirror in a riddle'.
Barth writes:

> The epiphany of Jesus Christ – the appearing of what has been done for us
> through Him, the disclosure of our life with Him as eternal life, the appearing
> of what we are . . . has not yet taken place . . . For that reason and to that
> extent our life under instructing grace is a waiting. But its reality is not
> diminished by the fact that we wait for the epiphany of Jesus Christ and of
> our life with him.

Simply because this life is concealed from our clear view does not mean it
is any less real. Christ has accomplished for us what we could not
accomplish for ourselves; Christ has taken our humanity into the heart of
God for us and has become for us all we are meant to be; Christ, by the
power of his Spirit, shares this life with us as we live together in this
community that lives by faith (not by sight). *We live*, in other words, *in
expectation of the fulfilment of that which has already been accomplished
for us in Christ*. 'Nor, again,' writes Barth, 'can we be more lavishly
endowed than we are already in this expectation . . . It is precisely in waiting
for His appearing that we shall be zealous unto good works.'[2]

A ministry through conflict recognises both the contingency of human
relationship and the fullness of God's being in communion. God uses the
stresses and tensions and the conflicts of human community to reshape us
into the image of Christ, an image that is not static, an image that is itself
communal and open-ended towards the future, God's future, which is for
us accomplished already in Christ. And this future is not a future in isolation,
but in the highest and most holy communion.

Christ reveals to us the dynamic being in communion of God, the
holy Trinity. God is, said G. K. Chesterton, himself a holy family.[3] This is
the image in which we are created and the life for which we are designed,
to live as Christ lived – as Christ lives for us – as Christ lives through us –
in the image of the God who pours out his life on behalf of 'the other'.

When we are in conflict, we do not see the ultimate goal of conflict as 'getting our own way'. Conflict is a means to an end, the end of our being transformed into the likeness of Christ. Conflict may raise for us issues of character. It almost certainly will expose to us (and to others) flaws in our character. These can be recognised and confessed; and consciously we may submit these flaws to God's healing grace. Conflict will allow us to hear others, to test our desires and their desires against one another in light of God's word. Conflict will allow us, on occasions, to know the rejection of others over those issues on which we must take a stand, and sometimes over no issues at all. Conflict, if viewed as an evil to be avoided or as an end in itself, can be disheartening and may lead us to the kind of exhausted emptiness we described earlier in our discussion of *vanity* (aka 'burnout'). But, if we can perceive God at work through conflict, we can offer ourselves and others to God, in the midst of conflict, trusting the outcome to God.

In a collection of essays, Carl Dudley presents a paper that touches on conflict. He discusses one way in which members of a congregation can grow (meaning, in this context, that they can come to a fuller understanding of the Church's mission and their place in that mission) through a process of reflecting on their vision of what it means to be the Church. Dudley, in other words, sees particular kinds of disagreements and conflicts as catalysts to Christian development.[4]

Unfortunately, such creative conflict is often short-circuited by pastors and other Church leaders who are so uncomfortable with disagreements and so fearful of conflict that they rush to resolve every murmur of discontent. This is done, frequently, in the name of the peace and harmony of the Church, when actually it is done primarily to preserve the comfort level of those in leadership.

The cross that stands at the centre of the Christian life is 'the emblem of suffering and shame', as the old hymn says. It is the emblem of death, but not death as an end in itself. We trust that God brings life from death and that God uses all of life to mould us into the likeness of Christ. Even while we must confess 'it has not appeared as yet what we shall be; we know that when he appears; we shall be like him', we also recognise that becoming like Christ involves purification, and this purification is a process which involves pain, not least the pain of interpersonal conflict.

Dante, in his *Purgatorio*, tells us that those who are being purified by the flames of God do not want to leave the flames until its purification is completed and they are fit for paradise. They are jealous of any time spent away from the flames of God's all-consuming love. St Paul moves the scene of this purgation from the realm of the afterlife to the here-and-now:

> Therefore having been justified by faith, we have peace with God through our Lord Jesus Christ, through whom we have also obtained our introduction by faith into this grace in which we stand; and we exult in hope of the glory of God. And not only this, but we also exult in our tribulations, knowing that tribulation brings perseverance; and perseverance, proven character; and proven character, hope; and hope does not disappoint, because the love of God has been poured out within our hearts through the Holy Spirit who was given to us (Romans 5:1–5).

Those of us who serve in the leadership of God's Church would do well to hear these words not only as true, but also as real. We lead through conflict towards the fullness of Christ.

Notes

1. Jürgen Moltmann, *The Church in the Power of the Spirit* (New York: Harper & Row, 1977). The parenthetical phrases corresponding to Moltmann's categories of 'Kingdom of God' and 'history' are drawn from Eberhard Jüngel, *Christ, Justice and Peace: Toward a Theology of State*, trans. D. Bruce Hamill and Alan J. Torrance, introductory essay by Alan J. Torrance (Edinburgh: T&T Clark, 1992), 70.
2. Karl Barth, *Church Dogmatics*, ed. G. W. Bromiley and T. F. Torrance, trans. G. W. Bromiley et al. (Edinburgh: T&T Clark, 1957), II.2.608.
3. G. K. Chesterton, *The Everlasting Man* (London: Hodder & Stoughton, 1925), 262.
4. Ellis Nelson (ed.), *Congregations: Their Power to Form and Transform* (Atlanta: John Knox, 1988), 89–113.

I need thee to teach me day by day, according to each day's opportunities and needs. Give me, O my Lord, that purity of conscience
which alone can receive, which alone can improve thy inspiration.
My ears are dull, so that I cannot hear thy voice. My eyes are dim, so
that I cannot see thy tokens. Thou alone canst quicken my hearing,
and purge my sight, and cleanse and renew my heart. Teach me to sit
at thy feet and to hear thy Word. Amen.

John Henry Newman

5

The Strength to Persist

The Ribbon of Steel

Carlyle Marney, one of the finest pastoral theologians in living memory, once asked why it is that ministers, the people who are supposed to be endowed with the confidence to storm the gates of hell, are so timid they can't say *boo*! to a church mouse. Marney warns us of an ailment that afflicts many of us who serve as leaders in the Church. Our failure to persist virtually guarantees ineffectiveness.

When I have opportunities to work with new ministers, one of the questions I inevitably ask them is this: 'Is there a ribbon of steel that runs through you and gives strength and persistence to your ministry?' The thing I'm trying to get at with this question is whether or not they have the courage to take a stand and stick to it. I want them to identity whether or not they can marshal the will not to run when they meet resistance. An uncertain trumpet, so we are told in the Bible, does little to rally the troops. And, uncertain, hesitant pastoral leadership – leadership that retreats at the first flash of conflict, leadership that changes positions and varies its direction at every criticism – is worse than no leadership at all.

The steel we need is like that of King Henry V when he stands before the tired and sick remnants of England's invasionary force against France, as imagined by Shakespeare in the famous St Crispin's Day speech prior to the battle of Agincourt, a speech that inspired a dispirited Britain pummelled by Hitler's bombs in the Second World War. When Lord Westmoreland wishes out loud that the English army had more soldiers to put in the field against the French, Henry responds by saying:

No faith, my coz, wish not a man from England: God's peace! I would not lose so great an honour, as one man more, methinks, would share from me for the best hope I have. O do not wish one more! Rather proclaim it, Westmoreland, through my host, that he which hath no stomach to this fight, let him depart; his passport shall be made, and crowns for convoy put into his purse: We would not die in that man's company that fears his fellowship to die with us . . . He that shall live this day, and see old age, will yearly on the vigil feast his neighbours, and say, Tomorrow is Saint Crispian: Then will he strip his sleeve and show his scars, and say, These wounds I had on Crispin's day . . . And gentlemen in England now a-bed shall think themselves accurs'd they were not here, and hold their manhoods cheap while any speaks that fought with us upon Saint Crispin's day. (Henry V, Act IV, Sc. III)

This is something of the quality of steel we need as pastors. The reason I've chosen the metaphor of a 'ribbon of steel' is because of the two qualities for which steel is best known: its flexibility and its strength. A ribbon of tempered steel can bend, and it can spring back into shape. It is flexible. But steel, even a ribbon of steel, is still steel. It is strong and clearly defined. It has sharp boundaries. It will probably cut me if I come up against it the wrong way. It resists breaking. Folded, forged and fired, steel represents the strength of swords and skyscrapers. At work, steel can outlast virtually any other material. Even at rest, steel supports and undergirds and defends.

'Is there a ribbon of steel running through me?' Is there a sense of who I am and what I stand for, what I value and what I hope? Do I have that internal focus of strength that enables me to know what is consequential and what is not, what can be negotiated away and what must remain in order for me to be who I am (come hell or high water)? Am I strong enough, as Kipling says, 'to hold on when there is nothing in you except the will which says . . . "Hold on!" '? And, when the time for rest is come, am I strong enough to rest, to be vulnerable, to let my creaturely weakness honour God by honouring God's Sabbath? *'Is there a ribbon of steel running*

through me?' This is the question which, finally, can only be asked *by* ourselves *of* ourselves; it must be asked *in the first person singular.*

A ribbon of steel should be standard equipment in all ministers. It isn't optional equipment. But, from what I can tell, 'the ribbon of steel' emerges in us slowly over years of experience and conflict as we are tempered in the fires of life, as we learn to define who we are, what we believe and what we value most. *All great leaders have this ribbon of steel running through them.* (Think for a moment, for example, about the ribbon of steel that ran through Winston Churchill, Abraham Lincoln, Martin Luther King Jr and Gandhi.)

Again, all great leaders possess it. *And all poor leaders lack it.*

Eugene H. Peterson discusses how important it is for the pastoral leader to have that strength of character which I call 'the ribbon of steel'. Peterson says that there are three elements of the minister's office that are non-negotiable: *prayer* (in response to the Word of God), *biblical and theological reflection* and the *spiritual direction* of the congregation (the pastor's participation in God's transformation of persons). He says that these activities are so vital, so difficult to carry out and so easy to get drawn away from *that we must be bound by the most solemn vows.*

Peterson alludes to an ancient Greek story to explain his thought; and, while he doesn't elaborate on the story, I want to tell it in full, though it is familiar. It is the story of Odysseus, the man who travelled the world and was tempered by life's adventures. At one point in his journey, as he and his men sailed the seas, they passed close to the island of the sirens. The sirens sang a beautiful song that lured ships onto the rocks. Sailors, it seemed, became captivated by the song of the sirens, drew closer and closer to the singers, until they crashed fatally onto the rocky island. Odysseus had heard of this happening. But he wanted to listen to the song. So he put wax into the ears of his sailors to prevent their hearing the siren voices. Thus, they could keep the boat on course. But he didn't put wax into his own ears. He told his men: 'You are to tie me up, tight as a splint, erect along the mast, lashed to the mast, and if I shout and beg to be untied, take more turns of the rope to muffle me.'

When we take our vows of ordination to Christian ministry, Peterson says, we are asking the Church to lash us to its mast with the most solemn promises we can make. We know we will hear the siren voices singing, luring us onto the rocks. Our culture is alive with siren voices, anxious, enticing, seductive voices, voices angry and blaming, voices claiming either that we must react to the surrounding anxiety or that we must run and hide. Voices from without and from within the Church entreat us to abandon the heart of this calling to ministry, or to redefine it in a way that is less offensive to certain social sensibilities and less threatening to the powers and principalities of our age.

Even the congregation we serve, from time to time, sings the siren song, especially if we are leading well. One day, a member of the congregation could come to any of us and demand that we tell them what they want to hear instead of what they need to hear. In the sacred vows we take, we promise ourselves, and God, and our congregation, that despite what we are asked to do later, we will not abandon our ship or (worse) steer it onto the rocks.

Peterson speaks (on behalf of the Church) to each of us who has taken or who will take these vows. He says:

> We are going to ordain you to this ministry and we want your vow that you will stick to it. This is not a temporary job but a way of life that we need lived out in our community ... Your task is to keep telling the basic story, representing the presence of the Spirit, insisting on the priority of God speaking the biblical words of command and promise and invitation.[1]

I want to reiterate what he is saying. *Even when the people don't want to hear that word, or want to deny that word, or apply it to someone else, or want to resist it with every fibre of their being, our responsibility is to keep*

on keeping on – and on – and on. Only those ministers who possess a
ribbon of steel can persist in this crucial task.

The question that stings like alcohol on a flesh wound is this: *'Is there a
ribbon of steel that runs through me?'* This is the question we ask ourselves
repeatedly. It is also the question our congregations ask us (mostly by
unspoken questions) again and again.

The minister's study can, and some days *will*, feel like a business office.
The demands for efficiency, for numerical expansion, greater efficiency,
and for the raising of funds will make themselves felt. Cravings for affection,
for confirmation of our culture's norms, for security and for some need
wrongly named 'comfort', will make themselves known in ways that could
compromise our calling. The voracious appetite for sociological relevance
can grow into a lust for conformity to the ways and means of the age. The
question that will not let us go when all these things happen is this simple
question: *'Is there a ribbon of steel that runs through me?'*

Over seventy years ago, a young minister named Karl Barth addressed
a group of ministers and told them why people came to church. His words
became a clarion call to his generation, and echo still today. He said that
on any given Sunday morning, when the bells ring calling the people to
worship, there is in the air an expectancy that something great, something
crucial, something momentous is going to happen. People, he said, come
to church wanting to know the answer to one question above all else: 'Is it
true?'

'And so they reach,' he said, 'not knowing what they do, towards the
unprecedented possibility of praying, of reading the Bible, of speaking,
hearing and singing of God.' They want to know the answer to this one
question, and not some other question that beats around the bush.

The latest techniques in Church management will not answer this
question. The newest books on personality theory, or the latest methods
for preaching a snappy sermon, won't answer this profound question. They
are driven by 'blood and tears, deepest despair and highest hope, a

passionate longing to lay hold . . . of him who overcomes the world because he is its Creator and Redeemer, its beginning and ending and Lord'. They must know, 'Is it true?'

They may, in fear and anxiety, actually try to restrain us from articulating the question of truth: it touches so deeply their awareness that what is falsely alive must die in the face of that which is truly Life. But, they will know that we have suffered a failure of nerve if we do not probe their wounds; they will know that we have failed more than them if we give them only something to deaden the pain and, in so doing, neglect to give them that which alone can heal. They will not thank us for allowing their anxiety to prevent us from dealing with the heart of the matter. They need us to lead them where they will not go on their own.[2]

Do we have backbone enough, I wonder, nerve enough, steel enough to be the ministers our people need? Ultimately this is a question each of us must answer in the presence of God. The answer, of course, is: *No, not by our own power.* But with God even this is possible.

Notes

1. Eugene H. Peterson, *Working the Angles: The Shape of Pastoral Integrity* (Grand Rapids: Eerdmans, 1989), 17–18.
2. Karl Barth, 'The Need and Promise of Christian Preaching', *The Word of God and the Word of Man* (Gloucester: Peter Smith, 1956), 104ff.

Thou loving Father, everything goes wrong for me and yet Thou art love. I have even failed in holding fast to this – that Thou art love, and yet Thou art love. Wherever I turn, the only thing that I cannot do without is that Thou art love, and that is why, even when I have not held fast to the faith that Thou art love, I believe that Thou dost permit through love that it should be so, O Infinite Love. Amen.

Søren Kierkegaard

6

The Joyful Ministry

to which God Calls Us

Basically, what we have said so far is that *the minister's activities are grounded, first, in the minister's character, and, second, in the mission of God's Church.*

The issues of *character* and *mission* are pre-eminently theological issues.

We are who we are because the God who created and redeemed us is the God revealed in the life, death and resurrection of Jesus Christ.

Our mission springs, in turn, from our understanding of who God is and what God is like.

If God were capricious, careening between acts of wickedness and deeds of arbitrary kindness, our mission might be to warn people to tiptoe through life terrified of their eternal destination, uncertain whether God can be trusted at any moment.

But, *if God is the God revealed in Jesus Christ*, the God who created all things from a wealth of unconditioned, unlimited, unbounded, unneedy love,[1] the God who abhors not the Virgin's womb, the God who at the cost of that which was most dear brought back to the Father's house those who were most unworthy, the God who loves creation so much that God will not rest until all creation shares the wholeness, completeness and perfection of God's eternal being-in-communion, *then our mission is quite different.*

The character of God and the mission on which God sends us determine the concrete shape of the pastor's ministry. We have been placed in congregations to contribute to the transformation of persons – nothing less!

Growth, the maturity of persons,
edification, transformation, conversion,
repentance, redemption, reconciliation
– *this is the goal, the ultimate outcome, the*
telos
towards which our faces are set like flint.
And *this* goal determines what
we shall do
– day-to-day, hour-to-hour –
as ministers.
Our mission, grounded in the character
of God, determines what activities we
will engage in, in what way,
and what activities we will refuse to
engage in, and why.

Irenaeus, the first great theologian of the Christian Church, wrote: 'Jesus Christ, in his infinite love, has become what we are, in order that he may make us entirely what he is.'

C. S. Lewis put it this way: '[T]he whole offer which Christianity makes is this: that we can, if we let God have His way, come to share in the life of Christ. If we do, we shall then be sharing a life which was begotten, not made, which always has existed and always will exist . . . The Son of God became a man to enable men to become sons of God.'[2]

This formula (which now sounds so gender-biased to my ears) enshrines the most basic teaching of the Church, what John Calvin called the *mirifica commutatio* ('the wonderful exchange'). Expanding on Calvin's thought, James Torrance has said:

Christ has come and taken our enmity, to give us love in exchange; our alienation and hostility; to give us his friendship in exchange; our sin, our condemnation, our death, to give us forgiveness, righteousness, and eternal life in exchange . . . The joyful ministry to which God has called us is to proclaim the good news of what God has done for us in Christ nineteen hundred years before we were born, and to summon people to receive Christ today with all the blessings that are treasured up for us in him.[3]

Now, *if* this really is what God is up to in and through the Church, and *if* this is the divine mission that gives shape to pastoral ministry, to announce the good news of what God already has done for humanity in Christ and, through the ministry of Word and Sacrament to participate in God's reconciliation of humanity in Christ and God's transformation of persons into the spitting image of Christ, *then* – in heaven's name – how can we be content to convert the pastorate into a gilded version of some corporate chief executive? Who could settle for manufacturing *widgets* when we are commissioned to make *disciples*?

St John Chrysostom (347–407), in his classic study, *On the Priesthood*, presents one of the most provocative portraits of pastoral ministry. Through a dialogue between two people, one of whom is attempting to avoid becoming a priest, Chrysostom explores the extraordinary mission in which God involves us as ministers of the gospel. At one point, about halfway through the treatise, Chrysostom has one of the partners in the dialogue say: 'The right course, I think, is to have so reverent an estimation of the office as to avoid its responsibility from the start.'[4] His words are reminiscent of what Pope Gregory I (known as Gregory the Great, 540–604) said to St Augustine of Canterbury, when Augustine set off to evangelise the English: 'It is better never to undertake any high enterprise than to abandon it when once begun.'[5]

These comments parallel Jesus' caution that those who lay their hand to the plough, but then look back, are not worthy of the kingdom of heaven. It is a caution we remember too little.

If 'the shepherd of souls' (as Chrysostom calls the minister) must be a person of wisdom and grace, character and cleanliness and possessing a quality even higher than any human goodness, 'then', he says, 'do not withhold your forgiveness from me' because I refuse to become one. Why should I 'want to damn myself without rhyme or reason?'[6] After all, everyone knows that the minister is, himself or herself, the real sermon, and his shortcomings (such as vanity, pride and gracelessness) 'simply cannot be concealed. On the contrary, even the most trivial soon gets known.'[7] After looking at the character required of those who occupy the office, the scope of the mission and the difficulty of the work, isn't it better simply to say, 'Thanks, *but no thanks*'?

Too seldom do we reflect on this advice. Many candidates for ministry tend to consider the ministry as a career requiring merely the mastery of a specialised set of skills and techniques. But, as the classic studies of the pastor's ministry (from Chrysostom to Richard Baxter) tell us, the ministry is a way of living in the midst of the people of God which persistently reminds us and the people of the priority of God's reign over our lives.

The greatest resource to pastoral care in antiquity was *Liber Regulae Pastoralis* of Gregory the Great.[8] This book, written c. AD 591, was translated and distributed by King Alfred of England. It became the guidebook for episcopal oversight throughout the medieval period. Gregory's book provided an excellent resource for reflection on transformational ministry.[9]

Gregory opens his *Pastoral Disipline* by saying that his purpose in writing is to describe how onerous are the burdens of pastoral ministry, 'so that he who is free from them may not imprudently seek to have them, and he who has been so imprudent as to seek them may feel apprehension in having them'. Gregory writes:

> No-one ventures to teach any art unless he has learned it after deep thought. With what rashness, then, would the pastoral office be undertaken by the unfit, seeing that the government of souls is the art of arts! For who does not realise that the wounds of the mind are more hidden than the internal wounds of the body? Yet, although those who have no knowledge of the powers of

drugs shrink from giving themselves out as physicians of the flesh, people
who are utterly ignorant of spiritual precepts are often not afraid of professing
themselves to be physicians of the heart, and though, by divine ordinance,
those now in the highest positions are disposed to show a regard for religion,
some there are who aspire to glory and esteem by an outward show of
authority within the holy Church. They crave to appear as teachers and covet
ascendancy over others, and, as the Truth attests: *They seek the first
salutations in the market place, the first places at feasts, and the first chairs
in the synagogues.*[10]

Gregory begins with a few words about the demands which ministry
makes on our capacity for knowledge and wisdom, our powers of insight,
perception, our ability to penetrate the mystery both of humanity and
divinity; *and* he includes a warning about going into ministry for the wrong
reasons and with the wrong expectations.

First, concerning the demands ministry makes on our knowledge and
wisdom: when I go in search of a doctor I look for one thing above all else,
his or her ability to diagnose and treat illness. Bedside manner, empathy,
ability to communicate a caring tone, all are secondary considerations. I'd
rather have a crude, rude and socially unacceptable person who, nonetheless,
can help me mobilise my immune system to fight off an infection than the
most kind, gentle, empathic 'Marcus Welby, MD' or 'Doctor Finlay'
imitator who can't figure out how to help my body get well.

The minister's task is not dissimilar to the work of the physician. It's
just a lot more difficult. The minister does need to communicate his or her
care for the congregation. Members of the congregation want and need to
know that the minister cares about and respects them as persons. We've
already noted this. But, as important as the minister's communication of
care and respect for the people is, the effective minister must also be able
to diagnose accurately what is going on in a congregation. The minister
must have extraordinary powers of observation, perception and critical
reflection. These diagnostic skills are all the more subtle and rare, because

the business of discerning what Gregory calls the hidden 'wounds of the mind' is more difficult than discerning the 'internal wounds of the body'.

The minister must be as good at therapeutic tactics as at diagnosis. The minister must know how to stimulate the immune system of a congregation to promote health and to inhibit all those factors that cause sickness. The effective minister leads the congregation from his own deep springs of spiritual health, communicating clearly the redemptive and transformative vision of the Christian faith, taking stands appropriate to this vision and hanging in there persistently to help the congregation become more healthy and better able to fight off the various pathologies, the malignancies and arteriosclerosis, the childhood diseases and common colds that afflict our life together.[11]

The best example of this quality of leadership, incidentally, is not to be found in corporations or political institutions, but in the New Testament. The Book of Acts, in particular, provides portraits on virtually every page of pastoral leadership at its finest, pastors who led from the depths of their own spiritual health, communicating clearly the redemptive and trans-formative vision of their common faith in the Risen Christ, taking stands appropriate to this vision and persistently trusting themselves and their success to God alone.

Understanding the significance and the difficulty of the minister's task, how could anyone undertake it without the most rigorous preparation and the commitment to a lifelong acquisition of knowledge and dedication to wisdom? And, yet, in virtually any city and town, you are likely to find those who feel completely qualified to hang out their sign as 'physicians of the heart', without blushing, though they'd never try to pass themselves off as mere 'physicians of the body'.

Second, concerning those who imprudently take on the task of pastoral ministry. We all have mixed motives. Even our *best* motives, *at best*, can march along shoulder-to-shoulder with motives so unworthy that we won't even admit to ourselves their existence; but, as Gregory reminds us, there is a grave danger in our going into the Ministry of Word and Sacrament *for the wrong reasons* and *with the wrong expectations.*

The ministry is, after all, an office of instructive leadership (hence in Presbyterianism the minister is designated 'Teaching Elder'). Pastoral leadership, by its very definition, assumes a context in which (1) there is a need for someone to take the lead, (2) there are those who will be led, and (3) conversely, there are those who will resist and sabotage leadership.

As we have already noted, conflict is inevitable, and even desirable, in this context. And those who are uncomfortable with conflict should avoid pastoral ministry. Those who are anxious about conflict, who do not have the courage to stand for those things essential to the mission of the Church, the grace to recognise when they are wrong, the humility to accept God's forgiveness, the stamina to persist over the long haul and the strength of character to entrust themselves and their ministry to God's hands – such people should avoid pastoral ministry, at all costs. It is not the right place either for those who want to pervert authority into tyranny or those whose insecurity and anxiety will not allow conflict and discomfort to emerge creatively among the people they are leading.

I am reminded, again, of the three essentials of leadership which Edwin Friedman describes: *clarity, non-anxious presence and the will to lead even in the face of resistance and sabotage.* Using these general categories from Friedman, let's attempt to answer the crucial question, 'What kind of leaders do our congregations need?'

(1) *Congregations need leaders who are able to articulate clearly the vision and the mission that emerge from their shared values and beliefs.* Good leaders, at times, bring to clarity the vision that lies dormant and unspoken among the people. Good leaders, at times, bring to remembrance the vision that lies at the foundation of the people's formation as a congregation or even deeper in the traditions that define who they are. Good leaders, at times, move ahead of the people

discerning the vision that is necessary for the future health of the people, while maintaining continuity with the congregation's heritage, with a view to bringing the people to share this new vision and to make necessary changes in the congregation so it can adapt to challenges in its environment.

In each case, the leader's ability to discern and the leader's ability to articulate clearly the vision of the people is crucial to the health of the congregation. For this reason, the leader must have a clear understanding of who he or she is, where he or she comes from, how his or her history informs or undercuts his or her ability to lead and what strengths lie hidden in his or her own history. A respect for personal, familial and institutional history is essential to leadership, because without this respect we are unable to articulate clearly the vision and the mission that emerge from our shared values and beliefs. William Faulkner once said: 'The past is not dead. *It isn't even past.*' Good ministers understand the significance of history and communicate their appreciation of the congregation's history to the people they lead.

(2) *Congregations need leaders who are 'in touch' and 'non-anxious'.* When anxiety chronically rules over us, *we lead poorly* (because we're preoccupied with survival), *we react* (as opposed to responding on the basis of considered reflection), *we blame* (as opposed to taking respon- sibility), *we play the victim* (and, in turn, victimise others), *and we avoid taking stands or making critical decisions.*

Anxiety has a way of stealing away those personal qualities we most need in order to lead effectively. I noticed recently how often in the gospels a heavenly messenger or, in some cases, Christ himself announced his presence with the words 'Fear not!' Good ministers embody a lack of anxiety, while poor ministers are driven largely by their anxiety, by fear of rejection, fear of outside forces, fear of society, of change, and of criticism, or the nameless, shapeless fear they 'catch' from other anxious people.

As ministers, we must remain close to the people we lead at all sorts of difficult moments, frequently in the most tense and potentially anxious situations of their lives (for example, birth, marriage, divorce, illness and death); and we must remain close while providing them a presence that is non-anxious. How many times have I stopped myself in the midst of a crisis (over a budget or some tragic illness) with the old Clinical Pastoral Education dictum: 'Don't just do something, stand there!' The minister's lack of anxiety steadies the congregation, allowing people to deal with the challenging situation at hand. The leader's non-anxiety is, in fact, the best immunisation to counteract the contagious nature of a congregation's anxiety.

Historians tell us that when the Roman legions first encountered Celtic tribes in battle, the relatively primitive Celts routed the better-trained and better-equipped Roman soldiers, largely with a single weapon – *panic*. The Romans simply had never before seen anything as terrifying as the Celts. The wild northern tribal fighters would rush the Roman lines. The Celts – naked, screaming, disorderly, tattooed, their hair bleached with lime standing straight up on end, in a chaotic frenzy of noise – would fall on the Roman lines as the Romans marched along. The Romans, in the first attacks, were terrified; they fell out of line and were slaughtered in their hundreds. In the end, it was non-anxious leadership that allowed the Romans to defeat the Celts and to go on, in time, to conquer most of Britain. The Roman leaders realised that if they could ignore the screams of the Celtic attackers and immediately go into the tight shield formations they had used successfully against other armies, they could defeat the unarmoured Celts. The Roman soldiers were taught, in essence, that if they conquered their own anxiety they would defeat their fierce opponents, and it worked. When the Romans refused to break ranks and run in terror, the Celts were defeated.

(3) *Congregations need ministers who will not cut and run in the face of resistance and sabotage.* Several years ago, James Dittes wrote a book titled *When the People Say No.* In that book, Dittes says:

To be a minister is to know the most searing grief and abandonment, daily and profoundly. To be a minister is to take as partners in solemn covenant those who are sure to renege. To be a minister is to commit, unavoidably, energy and passion, self and soul, to a people, to a vision of who they are born to be, to their readiness to share and live into that vision. To be a minister is to make that all-out, prodigal commitment to a people who cannot possibly sustain it. That is the nature of ministry, as it is of the God thus served.[12]

Ministry, Dittes tells us, is frequently lonely because the people do say 'No'. While we are almost totally committed to this ministry, involved – body and soul – in the life and mission of the Church of Jesus Christ, *for many church members it is just one among many other concerns competing for time, energy and interest.*

The Ministry of Word and Sacrament is not for the faint-hearted; it is for those who can live with and live through the loneliness, because it is often when the people say 'No' that our ministry has the opportunity to make real progress in their lives. It is a fact of our common humanity that we often resist most when a message is breaking through. It is, therefore, a common fact of leadership that *sabotage is part of the process of change.* Good leaders, far from dreading sabotage, look forward to dealing with it, because it tells them progress is being made. Effective ministers have the character necessary to get *to* and *through* the 'No' of the people even when standing virtually alone because they realise they are not called simply to be liked, but to lead. The most ineffective ministers are those who, for the sake of 'pleasing' others, refuse to lead, and in the end become utterly 'unlikeable'.

What I'm talking about here, of course, is not the megalomania of a minister who is so arrogantly preoccupied by his or her own agenda as to refuse to listen to the needs, concerns, criticisms and perspectives of others. *We need one another to keep us honest and on track. Good ministers, like all good leaders, listen.*

What I'm talking about is the minister who understands his or her own frailty and guards against the human tendency to tyranny by being thoroughly in touch with the people. But, when the tough decisions have to be made and stands have to be taken and leadership has to be given, this is the minister who is willing to pay the price to lead.

In this regard, the prayer of St Francis of Assisi provides a portrait of sane pastoral leadership. Francis prayed: 'O divine Master, grant that I may not so much seek to be consoled, as to console, to be understood, as to understand, to be loved, as to love. For it is in giving that we receive; it is in pardoning that we are pardoned; it is in dying that we are born to eternal life.'

Leadership preoccupied with its own survival fails because it, repeatedly, snatches defeat from the jaws of victory. We are never more effective as leaders than at the moment when the anxiety of the people compels them to say ' No further!' and we refuse to forsake either them or the costly goals before them. The good minister is able to stay close to the people, non-anxiously present with them, persistently and clearly articulating the values and the mission for which the congregation stands and on the basis of which they have embarked on the task ahead. Such pastoral leadership is, itself, the healing treatment Gregory says we are called to provide and that we must become knowledgeable enough and wise enough to provide. This is, in part, what Gregory means when, in the closing chapter of Part I of his *Pastoral Discipline*, he says: 'A man is lame who does, indeed, see the way he should go, but through infirmity of purpose is unable to follow persistently the way of life which he sees.'[13]

The strength required for this kind of persistence does not flow merely from the minister's personality. It flows, as John Calvin insists, from God's call. William J. Bouwsma observes that God, according to John Calvin, *calls persons individually to the ministry of the gospel*; 'they do not enter it, for motives of their own, voluntarily'. Calvin himself said: 'He alone deserves to be considered a legitimate minister of God and a prophet and teacher of the church . . . who is not impelled by his own flesh nor by an unconsidered zeal, but to whom God extends his hand and who simply obeys.' 'A minister is permitted in some things to be mistaken,' Bouwsma says, commenting on Calvin's assertion, 'but he must be certain of his calling; this certainty is the major source of his strength.'[14]

The second feature of Gregory's instructions on preparation for pastoral ministry warns that *'Those should not take on the office of governing* [pastoral leadership] *who do not fulfil in their way of life what they have learned by study.'*

'[T]here are some', Gregory writes, 'who investigate spiritual precepts with shrewd diligence, but in the life they live trample on what they have penetrated by their understanding. They hasten to teach what they have learned, not by practice, but by study, and belie in their conduct what they teach by words. Hence it is that when the pastor walks through steep places, the flock following him comes to a precipice.'[15]

It does no good (and, indeed, may do much harm) for the minister to preach a sermon series on 'Trusting God' based on the Sermon on the Mount, if it is clear during the so-called 'stewardship season' that his or her trust is in the manipulation and coercion of the congregation to reach certain fiscal objectives. The sermon preached gets drowned out by the much louder sermon lived.

For instance, we may bemoan the fact that ministers and their families live in glass houses, but trying to put up thicker curtains over the picture windows only contributes to the suspicion that something shameful is going on inside. Neither should this fact lead the minister to demand of his or her family an unforgiving and legalistic standard of behaviour which runs counter to the grace and mercy of the gospel. One of the best lessons any congregation can learn is that the health of the families in the congregation is one of the congregation's greatest assets; and this is best learned when the pastor leads by setting a priority of health for his or her own family, especially by making time simply to enjoy being with and playing with his or her spouse and children.

Another example: those who decide early in their ministries that the activities of the Church have precedence over the wisdom that prescribed a Sabbath for every human being send the message that their own compulsion is more sacred than the mercy of God. It tells the congregation that they do not respect the limits set on our humanity. And that is a message that carries its own damnation, as we see all too clearly in the consumerism of modern society that is consuming our energy, our time and the better part of our lives in the headlong pursuit of goods and services.

Gregory's next observation may take modern listeners a little by surprise. Maybe he took the ears of antiquity by surprise too. He writes:

> [W]ho could have exercised supreme domination over men so blamelessly as He whose rule would have been over subjects whom He had Himself created? But since He came in the flesh for the purpose of not only redeeming us by His Passion, but of teaching by His life, giving an example to those who follow Him, He would not be a king, but freely went to the gibbet of the Cross. He fled from the exalted glory offered Him and chose the pain of an ignominious death, that His members might learn to flee from the favours of the world, not to fear its terrors, to love adversity, for the sake of truth, to shrink from prosperity, for this latter thing often defiles the heart by vainglory, but the other cleanses it by sorrow . . . It is a common experience that in the school of adversity the heart is forced to discipline itself; but when a man has achieved supreme rule, it is once changed and puffed up by the experience of his high estate.[16]

What can we possibly say in comment on this passage? Ours is an age when the applause of many hands is taken infallibly to mean the rightness of any venture. Ours is an age when cost-effectiveness has been elevated to the status of canonical writ.

More important than this, however, ours is an age when adversity, difficulty and pain have ceased to be regarded as essential tools in the hands of a gracious God to fashion in us the mind of Jesus Christ, and have come to be regarded merely as aggravations which can be avoided with adequate long-range planning and managerial efficiency.

Gregory reminds us that the cross is not incidental, but central, to a proper understanding of pastoral ministry. The cross is not the result of miscalculation of certain political consequences, it is the very wisdom of God. Or, as Lesslie Newbigin has observed, the cross is not a 'defeat' which the resurrection had to reverse. The cross is God's victory on which God places His stamp of approval through resurrection. 'The King', he writes, 'reigns from the tree. The reign of God has indeed come upon us, and its sign is not a golden throne but a wooden cross.' The resurrection proclaims this fact.[17]

This was Alan Lewis's concern when he described Christian ministry as a *kenotic* ministry, our 'vocation in the *ecclesia crucis*', a ministry that is conformed to the shape of the God who 'emptied himself, taking the form of a bondslave, being born in human likeness. And being found in human form, he humbled himself and became obedient to the point of death – even death on a cross' (Philippians 2:7–8). Lewis wrote: 'Now if kenosis, divine self-emptying, truly is the means by which Christ's risen lordship is realized and God's Godness fulfilled, the friends and servants of Christ surely comprise an *"ecclesia crucis"*, a church of the cross – a kenotic community in Christ, participants through him in God's own kenotic ministry.'[18]

Gregory's next warning is valuable whether or not one decides to answer the call to the Ministry of Word and Sacrament. He says: 'Preoccupation with the governing of others dissipates the concentration of the mind.' He goes on to explain:

> Often it happens that when a man undertakes the cares of government, his heart is distracted with a diversity of things, and as his mind is divided among many interests and becomes confused he finds he is unfitted for any of them . . . [T]he mind cannot possibly concentrate on the pursuit of any

one matter when it is divided among many. When it permits itself to be drawn abroad by concerns intruding upon it, it empties itself of its steadying regard for the inmost self. It busies itself setting external matters in order, and, ignorant only of itself, it knows how to give thought to a multitude of concerns, without knowing its own self. For when it implicates itself more than is needful with what is external, it is as though it were so preoccupied during a journey as to forget what its destination was . . .[19]

One of the most enduring features of pastoral ministry is its stunning variety. Gregory noticed it 1,500 years ago. And any minister who has tried to juggle – *in one day* – a men's prayer breakfast, a Bible study with the Women's Mission Society, a conference with a school headteacher, two counselling sessions, an afterschool youth fellowship, a planning meeting with the architect for the new church hall and a community-wide meeting in the evening to discuss an outbreak of racist incidents which involve members of the congregation (on both sides of the conflict!) knows it is as true today as it was for St Gregory. The variety of tasks which present themselves to the pastor is one of the most exciting, enjoyable and stimulating aspects of ministry; but it is also one of ministry's most demanding and exhausting factors. For those who love variety, there's an endless supply. But there's also a danger in the variety, and Gregory has described it well: *We can become so 'preoccupied during the journey as to forget what its destination was'.*

Henri Nouwen, in perhaps his finest book, describes the busy, distracting, worry-filled lives we live. Then he says that Jesus does not respond to our busy lives by taking us out of this busy world. 'He does not try to pull us away from the many events, activities, and people that make up our lives. He does not tell us that what we do is unimportant, valueless or useless. Nor does he suggest that we should withdraw from our involvement and live quiet, restful lives removed from the struggles of the world.' Jesus' response to busy lives, he says, 'is quite different. He asks us to shift the point of gravity, to relocate the centre of our attention, to change our priorities. Jesus wants us to move from the "many things" to the "one necessary thing".'[20]

This is, essentially, Gregory's insight for us as well. And the implications of this insight for the quality of pastoral ministry are clear. The minister whose attention is not focused on that one necessary thing – the ultimate goal, the proper end, the final destination of Christian ministry – brings chaos to the congregation; while the minister whose spirit is nourished by the Word and Spirit and whose vision is fixed on God's ultimate purpose for ministry can bring to a multitude of activities a sense of 'centre', a quiet and strong quality of leadership which creates order out of chaos.

This is a dominant concern in the classics of pastoral formation. One of the most extraordinary pastors of all time, the Anglican divine George Herbert, understood each of the minister's days as governed by the order of a kind of holy rhythm in the midst of secular life, a balanced movement from Morning Prayers to Evening Prayers, as though the bells of his parish church called him constantly to a divine 'centre' beyond the day's activities. The characteristics of Morning and Evening Prayers in the Anglican Church are the reading and hearing of the Psalms and Scripture Lessons appropriate to the day, together with the responsive collects and intercessions. It is our attentiveness to the Word and our response to the Word in prayer that gives us our focus on the 'centre of unbroken praise', which brings coherence to our days.

Early in his *The Country Parson*, Herbert says that the Bible is not simply a source of information, professional or otherwise, for the minister. Rather it is 'the storehouse and magazine of life and comfort' which the pastor, like a baby, 'sucks and lives'.[21] The minister, as Herbert observes, is nourished by reading prayerfully and praying in reflection on the Word. The discipline of daily prayer and prayerful biblical reflection form the core of the minister's work, keeping the minister's focus on the one necessary thing, the kingdom of God, whose claim on us, as we have observed, is unambiguous in an ambiguous world.[22]

Gregory has other warnings, such as his warning for those who could benefit others by assuming pastoral leadership, but who selfishly refuse to do so in order to live quiet lives of study and reflection. One remembers John Calvin's attempt to do just that until he was confronted by William Farel, whereupon, under Farel's threat of calling down God's judgement on Calvin's head, Calvin hesitantly agreed to become the leader of the Reformation in Geneva.

Gregory has other warnings beyond the scope of our concern. But, finally, in Chapter 10 of Part I of the *Pastoral Discipline*, he summarises 'the character required of a man who comes to rule'. Gregory says: 'He, therefore – indeed, he precisely – must devote himself entirely to setting an ideal of living.'[23] Ministry, in other words, is engaging in a way of life among the people of God. Ministry is not simply something we do, the application, as it were, of various professional techniques, as though it were something we do on certain occasions and leave off on other occasions.

The fact that Gregory impresses on his reader more than any other is that the integrity of our ministry is directly tied to our personal authenticity. A minister is something we become, someone we are. Vocation is fundamentally related to being.

Eugene Peterson, in a series of lectures in 1993, said that the professional techniques we need to master as ministers can be mastered in a few years. However, the difficult part of pastoral ministry is not the mastering of professional techniques; it is being faithfully human. And being faithfully human has to be tackled afresh every morning of our lives.

Peterson is fundamentally right. He does not minimise the considerable skills that every minister must master in every area from biblical translation to organisational management. All of these are important. But, the greatest challenge the minister faces is coming to terms with our humanity under the call of God and God's Church, coming to terms with who we are and what God expects of us and what others expect of us in the name of God. This is the difficult part. But it is the most important part; it is the crucial task of ministry: coming to terms with the cross of Jesus Christ as the very centre point of the universe on which hangs our failure and our future, our sin and our redemption, our death and our hope. It is the tormented figure on the cross, this man from Nazareth, this God made flesh, who makes sense of who we are and who identifies us among humanity, giving us the only authority that matters as pastors.

This is the hardest part. And it's the first part and the final end of ministry. If we don't build on this foundation, our whole ministry is built on sand, because ministry that follows in the way of the cross is the only ministry which can lay claim to the adjectival modifier 'Christian', because the only Christ we have is crucified.

Notes

1. Classically, this is referred to as 'divine aseity'. See Thomas Merton, *The Seven Storey Mountain* (New York: Harcourt Brace Jovanovich, 1948), 172–3, for the practical implications of this doctrine.
2. C. S. Lewis, *Mere Christianity* (London: Collins, 1952), 150.
3. James B. Torrance, 'The Ministry of Reconciliation Today: The Realism of Grace', in Christian D. Kettler and Todd H. Speidell (eds), *Incarnational Ministry* (Colorado Springs: Helmers & Howard, 1990), 130–1.
4. St John Chrysostom, *On the Priesthood*, trans. Graham Neville (Crestwood, New York: St Vladimir's Seminary Press, 1984), III.10.
5. Bede, *A History of the English Church and People*, trans. Leo Sherley-Price, rev. R. E. Latham (London: Penguin, 1968), 67.
6. Chrysostom, *Priesthood*, III.7
7. Ibid., III.14.
8. Sometimes translated as *Pastoral Care*, or *Pastoral Rule*, or, as Stanley Hall translates the title, *Pastoral Discipline*. The edition used here is the excellent translation by Henry Davis, SJ, published as Volume II in the 'Ancient Christian Writers' series (New York: Newman Press, 1950).
9. There are a number of classical sources for pastoral ministry, including, also from the fourth century, Gregory of Nazianzus' 'Oration II: In Defence of his Flight to Pontus', the great seventeenth-century classic by George Herbert, *The Country Parson*, Richard Baxter, *The Reformed Pastor*, and the twentieth-century classic by Reinhold Niebuhr,

Leaves from the Notebook of a Tamed Cynic, among others. I recommend that we allow them to become partners in our ongoing conversation concerning our own practice of ministry and living resources for theological, personal and spiritual reflection at all times, but especially in times of conflict or pain.

10. Gregory, *Regulae Pastoralis*, trans. Davis, I.1.
11. I am particularly indebted to Murray Bowen's 'Natural Systems Theory', as seen in both Edwin Friedman and Michael Kerr, for the essential insights concerning the stimulation of the congregations' immunological system.
12. James E. Dittes, *When the People Say No* (New York: Harper & Row, 1979), 1.
13. Gregory, *Regulae Pastoralis*, I.11.
14. Bouwsma's lecture appears in the monograph, *Ministry in the Life of the Reformed Church Today: Papers Presented at a Colloquium in Honor of John Haddon Leith*, ed. Charles E. Raynal, Union Theological Seminary, Richmond, Virginia, 3–4 April 1989.
15. Gregory, *Regulae Pastoralis*, I.2.
16. Ibid., I.3.
17. Lesslie Newbigin, *Foolishness to the Greeks: The Gospel and Western Culture* (London: SPCK, 1986), 127.
18. Alan E. Lewis, 'Unmasking Idolatries: Vocation in the *Ecclesia Crucis*', in *International Ministry: The Presence of Christ in Church, Society, and Family*, 111.
19. Gregory, *Regulae Pastoralis*, I.4.
20. Henri Nouwen, *Making All Things New* (New York: Harper & Row, 1981), 41–2.
21. George Herbert, *The Country Parson, The Temple*, ed. John N. Wall Jr (New York: Paulist Press, 1981), 58.
22. Eberhard Jüngel, *Christ, Justice and Peace*, 70.
23. Gregory, *Regulae Pastoralis*, I.10.

Conclusion

This book began with a more-or-less humorous anecdote about pastoral image and the disjunction between the expectations of 'the age' and the call to follow Christ into the way of the cross. We shall close by returning to our opening question, 'How should we look if we are supposed to reflect the image of the God who has revealed himself to us in the tormented shape of a Jewish man named Jesus, crucified on a city dump and discarded by the powers of his world?' What would our ministry look like, in other words, if we decided to follow Christ into the midst of this God-crucifying world, with the love and grace and mercy which Christ incarnated and the will to work through the pain and suffering of this world to God's ends? This is the call of ministry, not to idealism (we are not imagining for one moment that the world rewards such behaviour), nor to escapism (the call to ministry is not the call to flee from the world, but the call to be in it). This is the call to transformational ministry, a quality of ministry that finds in the cross of Christ the revelation of the God who has his very being in communion and who, in communion, pours out his life and love eternally, and that through the power of the crucified Christ shares in the life and love of this God poured out for the world.

Thus I close this book with a prayer.

> Deliver us, O Lord,
> from optimism,
> that we may learn not to place our trust in things,
> but in you.

55

Deliver us, O God,
>   from romanticism,
>   that we may content ourselves with your creation,
>   rather than the fantasies of our own minds.

Deliver us, we pray,
>   from naïveté,
>   that we may embrace the maturity
>   to which you call us.

Deliver us, O Christ,
>   from idealism,
>   that we may come to love the real world you created
>   and for which you gave your life.